SMART BRAIN RIGHT BRAIN

An Introduction to Numbers and Shapes

Om KIDZ
An imprint of Om Books International

First Published in 2021 by

Om KIDZ | Om Books International

Corporate & Editorial Office
A-12, Sector 64, Noida 201 301
Uttar Pradesh, India
Phone: +91 120 477 4100
Email: editorial@ombooks.com
Website: www.ombooksinternational.com

Sales Office
107, Ansari Road, Darya Ganj
New Delhi 110 002, India
Phone: +91 11 4000 9000
Email: sales@ombooks.com

Author: Shweta Sinha
Editor: Kirti Pathak
Art & Design: Anshuman Pandey, Gaurav Bhandari, Harish Arya

ISBN: 978-93-5276-854-7

Printed in India

10 9 8 7 6 5 4 3 2 1

CONTENTS

1. I Can Count

This is Carla's room. What things can you see in her room?

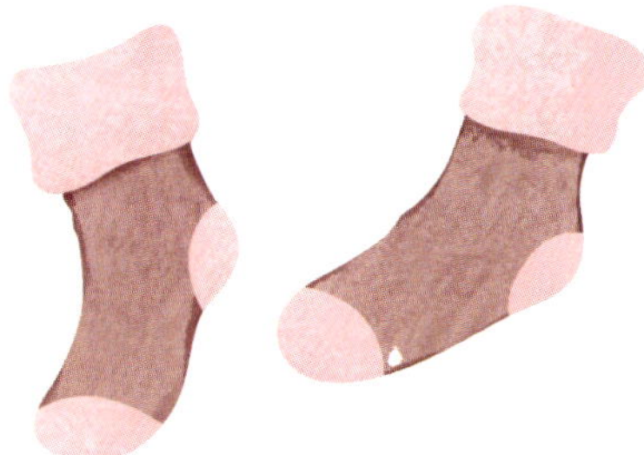

POCKET FACT

A 'pair' is two things that go together. We wear a pair of socks.

Carla loves to play in the park. Count these in the park-

6 trees

7 children

8 birds

9 flowers

10 balloons

2. Counting with Fingers

Carla counts with her fingers. Can you count with yours?

Close your fist. How many fingers do you see? You do not see any fingers. You see **0** fingers.

Stick out a finger. This is **1** finger.

Stick out more fingers and keep counting- **2, 3, 4, 5**.

DID YOU KNOW?

The number 0 looks like an egg. 0 means nothing.

Carla loves counting so much, she uses both her hands to count.

How old are you? Count your age on your fingers.

POCKET FACT

For a countdown of 10, you have to count backwards from 10 to 0.

3. 1-Digit, 2-Digits

0, 1, 2, 3, 4, 5, 6, 7, 8 and 9 are also called 'Digits'. We put digits together to make other numbers. Putting together '1' and '0' makes '10'.

Number 10

DID YOU KNOW?

Number 10 is made of 2 digits. So, it is called a '2-digit' number.

What happens if you place a '0' before 1?

0 1 gives us 1.

$$\underbrace{0 \quad 1}_{\text{Number } \mathbf{1}}$$

Placing 0 before another digit does not make a new number.

0 2 gives us 2.

0 3 gives us 3.

0 4 gives us 4.

Quiz

What will '0' and '5' give us?

0 5 gives us _____

4. Making More Numbers

Let's make more 2-digit numbers.

11 puppies

11 players make up a soccer, a cricket and a field hockey team.

A group of 12 is also called a dozen.

A dozen flowers

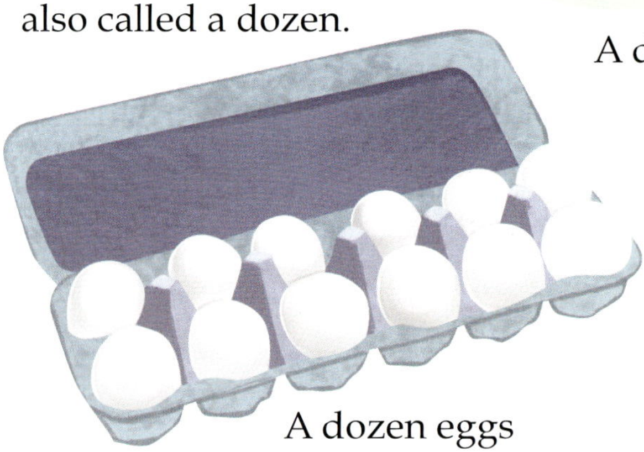

A dozen eggs

DID YOU KNOW?

There are 12 months in a year.

13

You become a teenager at age 13.

13 pencils

DID YOU KNOW?

A group of 13 is called a baker's dozen.

14

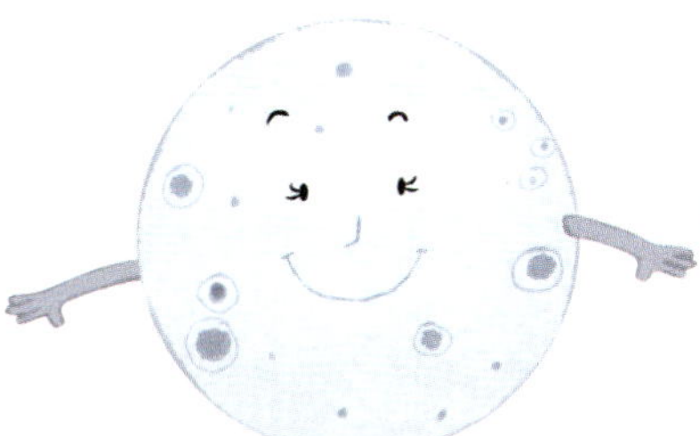

14 birds

The moon takes 14 days to go from new moon to full moon. It takes another 14 days to go back from full moon to new moon.

POCKET FACT

14th October is celebrated as World Maths Day.

15

15 is the first point you win in a game of tennis.

15 apples

16

In many countries you can get a beginner's driving license at age 16.

16 candles

DID YOU KNOW?

Most caterpillars have 16 legs. But when they emerge as a butterfly or a moth, they have only 6 legs.

17

The letter 'Q' is the 17th letter in the English alphabet.

17 fishes

18

18 cupcakes

POCKET FACT

In most countries you become an adult at 18 years of age.

19

Numbers from 13 to 19 are called 'teen' numbers.

19 stars

20 ladybugs

20

In a game of 20 questions, you have to identify an object by asking up to 20 questions.

POCKET FACT

If the eye doctor says you have 20/20 vision, it means you don't need glasses.

5. Activity: Count the dots and guess the number.

6. Bigger and Bigger

There are **24** hours in a day. Each hour has **60** minutes. And each minute has **60** seconds.

February is the shortest month with **28** days.

A standard monopoly board has **40** spaces.

There are **7** days in a week.

There are **52** weeks in a year.

Divide 50-50 is to split something into two equal parts.

There are 88 keys in a piano.

99 is the biggest 2-digit number.

7. The Big 100

100 is made of 3 digits - 1, 0 and 0. So, it is a 3-digit number.

A century is a 100 years.

Cats make a 100 different sounds.

There are numbers bigger than 100 too!

1,000
a thousand

1,000,000
a million

1000,000,000
a billion

1,000,000,000,000
a trillion

What is bigger than a trillion?

A quadrillion, a quintillion, a sextillion, a septillion

DID YOU KNOW?

A googol is '1' followed by a 100 zeroes!

8. A Numbers Game

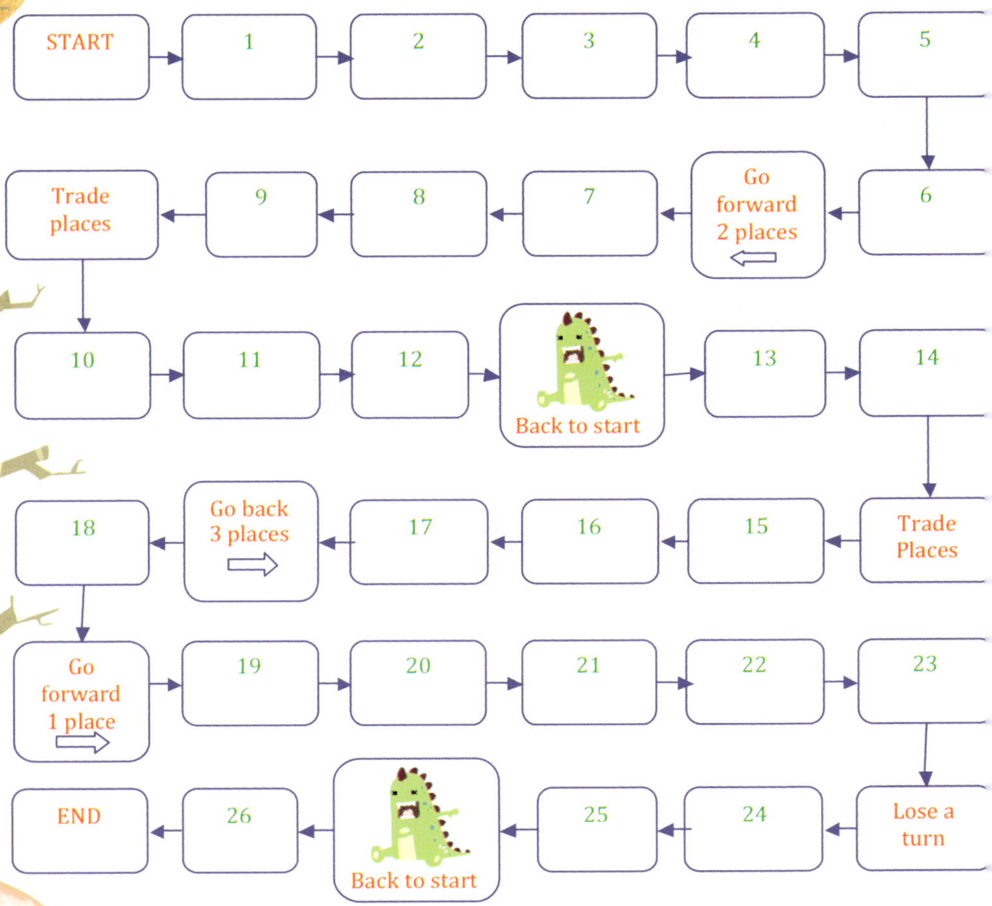

Rules to Play:

• You need: A playing coin for each player and a dice.

• Roll the dice and move your coin the number of places on the dice.

• Lose a turn: the player loses a turn to play.

• Go forward/Go backward as the square says

• The Dragon square, sends you back to start.

• Trade Places: Swap places with an opponent.

• To finish, you must get the exact number to END. If you have more, count forward and backwards. For example if you are at 26, you need 1 on the dice. If you get 4, count forward to END, then 3 backwards to 25.

9. Shapes

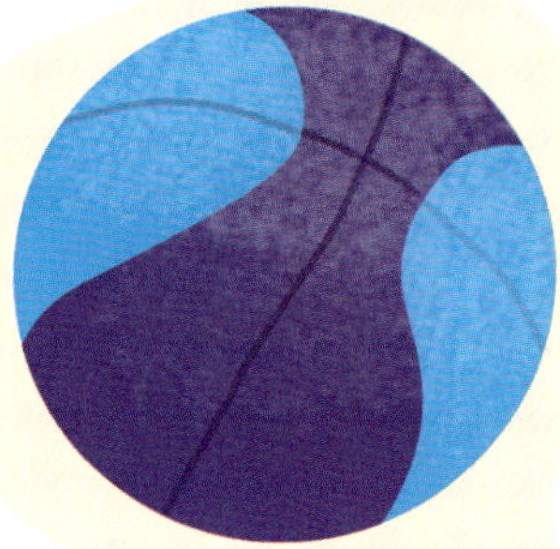

Circle

A circle is round like the letter 'O'

DID YOU KNOW? A doughnut is shaped like a circle. The hole at its centre is also a circle.

The sharpened end of a pencil is a triangle-shape.

A triangle has three corners.

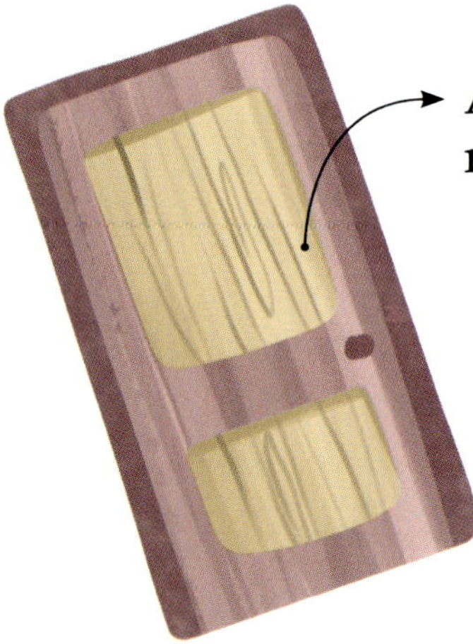

All doors are rectangle-shaped.

A rectangle has four sides.

The rectangle-shaped bus has circle-shaped wheels.

DID YOU KNOW?

The sides of a rectangle are straight lines.

A chessboard has 32 white squares and 32 black squares.

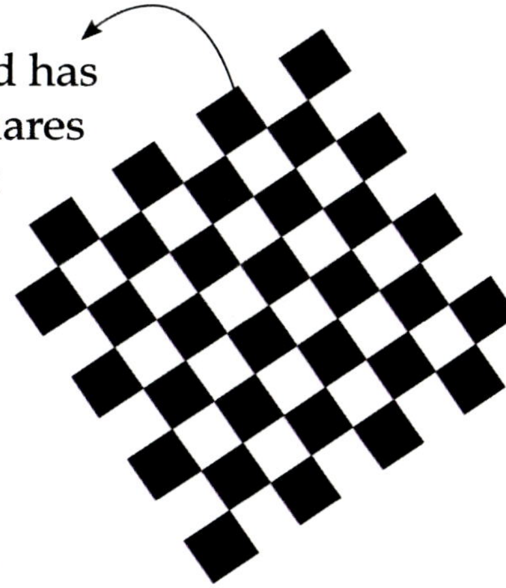

Make a square by sticking four popsicle sticks together like this.

Square

All sides have the same length.

POCKET FACT

A square is a rectangle with four equal sides.

The number zero is an oval.

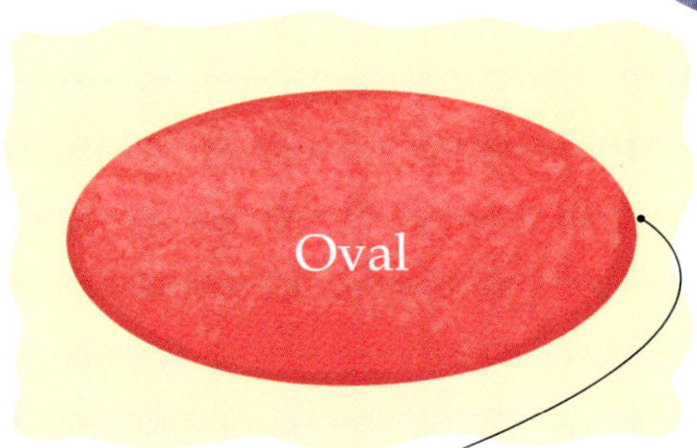

An oval has curved sides.

POCKET FACT

If you stretch a circle from opposite ends, you get an oval shape.

People use a surfboard to ride the sea waves.

Other Shapes

A starfish looks like a star.

A kite has a diamond-shape.

Heart-shaped strawberries.

Let's Get Active

Count the pictures

Count the pictures and circle the correct number from the options below.

7 8

4 5

3 2

5 6

Count and Match

Count the number of pictures in each group and match with the correct number.

	11
	15
	13
	8
	3

Circle all the 2-digit numbers here.

11	2	57
100	10	1000
4	0	22